Data Proficiency for Small Businesses

Driving Growth through Business Intelligence

J. Mary Eden

Table of Contents

Introduction 5
Problem description 7
Objectives of Study 10
Small and Medium Enterprises 13
Analysis methodology 15
Organization of the dissertation 18
As components from Business Intelligence 20
Data Warehousing 23
Data Warehouse Architecture 26
Analytical process 28
    Originally, the analytical process was designated 28
    Viewing of dice 29
General and analytical accounting 34
The Balance 38
Demonstration of Results 40
    Generally accepted accounting principles 40
    Organized or not, if the organizations are obligated to 41
Financial analysis 43
The financial balance; 44
    - Or growth; 44
    - Or I'm sorry. 44
    Ratios 45

Like seam: 46

Financial considerations 48

Operational reasons 50

Data Warehousing Process 56

Modeling of accounting data..59

Data Warehouse Architecture 61

Critical factors of success..68

Strategic alignment..70

Definition of objectives and goals................................73

Reactive focus 76

Proactive focus 77

Applicability of the prototype not yet decided............79

Analysis and definition of metrics...............................81

Checking the results..82

Validation methodology 83

Process interveners 84

Investigation questions...88

Official information on organizational management....89

Results of the questionnaire......................................90

Association das Equines e Medias Businesses.............91

    Orem dos Technical Officials de Contras 95

National Association of Young Entrepreneurs.............98

Conclusions and recommendations..........................101

Introduction

Business information is considered an elevated asset imports regardless of organizational size. No Within its activity, there is no production process, no contact with bakers and customers or at any other stage, as organizations germ data that could be subsequently sorted out and used for different purposes. The recording of accounting data is not a recent practice, in fact it dates back to the time when the commercial truces began 2000 years BC, passing by the Romans and Gregory's who ate there Egyptian civilization Egyptian.

The first vestiges of the act of establishing a control system, even as a rudimentary form, we go back to 8000 years.

Empirical accounting practiced in that era was a symbolic one that combined the figurative with the numerical. More lately, in the average world, the accounting system was relegated due to the collapse of the Roman Empire, the invasion of the German.

In Modern Date, starting from the 15th century establishment of new marine wheels, three increments from commercial activity, which is a technical expansion.

I register the counts, following the technique of the "double the "parts. No century XVIII we were inspired by the first accounting schools in England that led to a greater dissemination and uniformed of accounting recording techniques, which continues throughout our days.

Problem description

As small and medium-sized businesses (PME), no pressure on your part legal and periodic obligation to provide accounting information to State and their subscribers, they are unaware of the potential of this information as an integral element of the companies' analytical component.

Normally, and regardless of organizational size, it is

Common organizations can include accounting records that reflect all current operations from economic.

For this reason, further use of accounting information for part of the organizations, which are obliged to request this information from Official Accounts Technician (TOC), starting from his/her communication

To bank entities, there is no request or maintenance of bank financing. In fact, it is normal practice among institutions financers request balances and blankets to their clients who allow us to analyze the evolution of the organization and responder consistent with the risk of credit.

The accounting information is provided with different data relating to its operational and financial component of activities, products, business units, processes, services and organizational customers.

For this reason, further use of accounting information for part of the organizations, which are obliged to request this information from Official Accounts Technician (TOC), starting from his/her communication

To bank entities, there is no request or maintenance of Bank financing. In fact, it is normal practice among institutions financers solicitude balances and blankets to their clients who allow us to analyze the evolution of the organization and responder consistent with the risk.

The accounting information is provided with different data relating to its operational and financial component of activities, products, business units, processes, services and organizational customers.

Proem, the relationship of data as factors ballistics. Through the incorporation of the techniques and procedures that we allow transform the finance demonstrations of the farm to constitute a more relevant value for the generalization of the organizations, if it is decision making, look at the formulation of extraction and planning of lingo prize.

Oh yes, in decisions associated with the attribution of resources that we allow establish our customers our products and our fixation policies prices, endorsement of with drawl from the organization and its collaborators, no organization of activities and planning of customers. Moldavia, a great deal of accounting applications still do not have analytical options available to explore the information in depth accounting, number of formats possible to analyze, which simultaneously incorporates the best media support decision in the expression of strategies, or that of a certain form delayed analysis of this information by the PME.

On the other hand, a general description of the accounting applications for the collection of accounting elements is essentially suitable to respond promptly to the State, or what time relegated to according to the plan or interest of the information in the analytical component,

And it is the perspective that this analysis will focus on, procuring beware of the interest in observing current accounting information multidimensional evolutionary perspective, with the intuition to propose and support strategic decisions in organizations.

Objectives of Study

This is absent in the possibility of small and medium items organizations will draw on the accounting information of this available, to adopt a set of management medicines strategy that goes towards some practical aspects of the analytical component, not within the scope of Business Intelligence (BI). One of the keys to business strategy for creating competitive advantages is to understand the facts you need organize your activities, this is what you expect provide small and medium businesses with the opportunity we understand the importance of information provided to you, starting from the accounting data to manage the trading processes at an strategic level.

our managers or recognize their potential information does not support decision-making.

In a general way, the realize action of small and medium businesses (PME), I have this information accounting and finance, because this is obligated for reasons taxes, not always done well by the same person for business purposes.

Accounting information, for the rest a clearly important component for organizations, it will be possible to provide a combination of economic metrics and financers to whom PME may not be able to give the desired relief. This study will be explored or potentially measured by you presentation of a prototype that highlights the importance these indicators for the management of the PME, and consequently may inform our managers or recognize their potential information does not support decision-making.

The recognition of the importance of the accounting data comes from the formulation of the PME strategy and, on the other hand, the extraction of this information, the stimulation or development of a prototype that demonstrate interest in accounting data.

Available in a more appetizing form and which would provide, me simultaneous analytical exploration of this information, as is possible get through the Business Intelligence hardware.

Demonstrators financiers podrida constituent for the manager of the SMEs a facilitating factor in the interpretation of the counts, at the same time that provides another level of understanding from its own business reality. It is an expectation that it will be analyzed and interpreted.

This results in strategic planning and decision making different.

☐

Small and Medium Enterprises

The target universe of the study consists of Small and Medium Enterprises (SMEs), as defined by the European Commission's standard 2003/361/EC of May 6, 2003. According to this definition, SMEs have between 10 and 249 employees, and their trading volume ranges from 2 to 50 million Euros. For all the features linked to the number of operators.

Trading volume or total assets is another parameter that is stratified organizational classification. At PME, there are some aspects that impress these companies' great groups, specifically:

Naps PME, the managers are confused with the shareholders; generally there is an echelon and organizational structure simple, with little or no delegation of power decision by the manager.

Predominance of companies with high-quality capital;

Your material, financial and human resources relatively small (in comparison with larger ones companies) or which creates, sometimes, limitations on access to

The area of operation of the PME is predominantly technology and organizational structures are more demanding, making it harder to find technicians or managers who are more specialized and should probably be paid more;

The PME's ability to trade is typically limited to the bank, even for large-scale bakers and clients of a certain size;

The PME's principal operational region is regional national, ongoing, in the current context of economic globalization; many are starting or reinforcing its internationalization.

Offer of Business Intelligence (BI) solutions for the EM segment this. The focus of the distributors of BI solutions is, and continues now, our large-scale businesses are bigger flexibility of the organization to support projects of this nature, and also for the financial capacity associated with its size, or which is delaying the offering of this solution to PME.

Analysis methodology

The analysis methodology is missing from the identification of the main principles proposed elements of study. To realize this present you are it is necessary to analyze in the first instance all the potentialities it has Business Intelligence (BI), according to the methodology, or strength and limitations, strong points and fragilities, and its adaptability to the context of small and medium businesses nationals.

According to the prerequisite I am trying to understand these main concerns at the level of business information. Recognize which business segments, activities, and areas warrant further investigation. Now select these segment small and medium enterprises (PME), a sinuous-se analysis perception and identification by nature of the obstacles that prevent companies from adopting BI practices in their business processes.

In this part of the analysis an investigation was carried out around bibliography as a form of support and complementary study.

Now the identification of the business segment, such as PME, is necessary understand the areas in which this study can be seriously implemented,

And these are the areas where it is seriously possible to obtain information from someone systematized and uniform zed form, habitually existents all as organizations. To the student I went over the accounting area, which facilitated the beginning of studying once I was around your area. To analyze the different components of accounting, Demonstrators financers, taxation e analyze financier naps organizations; allow us to demonstrate its great potential information does not support decisions and formulation of extraction strategies long time for the organizations.

However, once you have learned to import the accounting data and from BI, the interconnection between both will be made easier with the existence of a prototype that demonstrates this interconnection in practice.

If I heard it, it was necessary to formulate a strategy for what it was claim and an action plan for your development. Deeds a requested information, passing through the support platform prototype, in the form of access to the prototype, as bases of dice, as unwinding hardware available and definition of the necessary skills for complete unwinding of the prototype, for the purpose of exhaustive planning.

Finally, after the devolution of the prototype, it is seriously necessary proceed with its validation, as seriously as this validation is carried out and that entities we can carry out this validation. Me conjunction into come orienteer, decide on the realization of the sights, on the location of some questions to some recognized public organizations that we can endorse and provide contributions for the prototype, for a application from BI to PME and to ensure reliability of accounting information, among other nature information particular do I study. Finished the trial of interviews, due-start writing the dissertation.

☐

Organization of the dissertation

The dissertation structure is divided into seven chapters. The first part is presented by thesis, focusing on the description of the problem, or objectively by its analysis, or the universe of the organizations Covered in the shield and the methodology to follow Chapter 2 is dedicated to describing the components of Business Intelligence in the PME, supported by a bibliographic review. Here are the different elements that can be applied to small and medium-sized organizations. Chapter 3 presents an analysis of the economic components and finances of an organization, accompanied by some practical examples. Ember or theme sea sample, look for yourself systematize alert to the importance of analyzing the organization's accounts, at the same time as carrying out a detailed analysis of the information with the information identified starting from the accounts. In chapter 4, here's a brief overview of Business Intelligence and the importance of carrying out an accompaniment to them economic-financial accounts and policies of an organization, establishment if a question of the two themes in the illustration of a Prototype.

In this part we will provide a practical example that highlights the application of counting and operations using some Business Intelligence concepts. prototype foe.

No chapter 5 explains the analysis of the different steps in the formulation from business strategy, implementation from Business Intelligence and how to organize this journey. Explicit-sea the importance of being able to have a well-defined strategy and objectives the PME and how the organization should be raised to support it option.

The methods utilized to verify the feasibility of carrying out the inquiry is the focus of Chapter 6. Choose two people and fill out the form as it was completed. Contacts forum fulcra are in the dissertation. The organization of these investigative questions prompted a critical analysis, so that the summer interviews motivated to make their contribution and simultaneously not return too extensor. The experience of the demonstrated interviews will be a preponderant factor in the investigation carried out.

Finally, the last chapter presents a conclusion to this study realized and as recommended for future work.

As components from Business Intelligence

Quoting a very concise phrase from Charles Darwin (1809-1882) concerning the importance of adaptation:

"The evolution of things is not the strongest that we live by even more quickly we adapt to the changes"

Globalization imposes new regress on business businesses. TO The variety of economies involved requires the integration of a management flexible on one side and, on the other, the decision-making process at the end of the performance impresario.

There have been several years since we have noticed the great organizations of the existing data in our systems, calculation instructions, bases scattered data, among others, and how we can invest in analytical systems, named Business Intelligence (BI). As PME has been, very recently, out of this concept and how we are going to reunite all, or even fewer, foods, as conditions for pondered welcome BI no longer from your organization.

Scattered data, among others, and how we can invest in analytical systems, named Business Intelligence (BI). As PME has been, very recently, out of this concept and how we are going to reunite all, or even fewer, foods, as conditions for pondered welcome BI no longer from your organization.

Some authors, such as Legendre (2005), The Gangadhara and Swami (2004), considers that BI cannot be applied to small and medium-sized businesses (PMEs) and that this is a process of managing the exclusive domain of large businesses. However, the PME is sureties as the same circumstances that motivate large organizations to systematize BI within their own organizations.

The term Business Intelligence (BI) was referred to by Hans Peter Lehn (1896-1964) to define as "the ability to learn as relationships of the facts presented in order to guide the action for an objective claim". More recently, in 1989, Howard Dresdner, analyst from Gartner Group, proposed BI as a thermo abrasive to describe "concepts and methods to improve your health business decisions supported in appropriate systems". Umea Recently defined by BI Aponte Para coverage ad architecture, hardware, given bases, applications and methodology

(Raising2004), with the objective of allowing access interact with the dice (for several times in real time) and allow them to right handling to supply business managers and analysts capable of carrying out an adequate analysis .

For Hill and Scott (2004), the essence of BI involves integration from relevant information such as the objective of detecting events or events significant considerations for the gesture. Which includes monitoring the evolution of business, the need to evolve and adapt quickly to new situations, if necessary and be informed about decisions?

Generally, BI is the evolutionary process that the data is sureties from its original form to its transformation Information that is then converted into knowledge. The data represents raw material (OLTP), which involves the selection, transformation and incorporation of summarization techniques (ETL)

They will be armed on the system's own dice and table bases de analysis (Data Warehouse), giving different interested parties a knowledge to mains enlarged of the data, at raves des armadas Analytical system techniques and visualization of the memos.

Data Warehousing

The Thermo Data Warehouse describes a repository of Oriented data poor assumed, integrated, historical and not volatile as time, as or objective of supporting the decision making process (Inman, 2005). Puma more detailed form; a Data Warehouse is a repository of

Data which includes the following characteristics:

Oriented by hiring, demonstrates the organization that

Describes the structure of the data, with the aim of facilitating the analysis of business de-emphasis, to the detriment of organization of the operational structure that is present orientation for the business process;

- Integrated, it wants to establish concentration and to organize by a single source of data;

- Historic, cohere a importance and analyze temporal ad information evolution;

- No dice when inserted into the dice bases,

It must not be the subject of actual discussion, but

Contrary to the operating dice bases that are suitable for you systemic alterations.

Building a Data Warehouse is an important business option, as it is a task that will involve everyone

Organization, and on the other hand involves an investment flow consider, what is in my materials, what is in my humans. TO finalization of the construction of the Data Warehouse is normally enlarged, or it will be possible to encourage any organization to give and I step in front of the right direction.

Don't worry about the architecture of the Data Warehouse, that's it normally associated with a top-down distribution, or meaning that,

Once constructed, it is possible to fragment into parcels

Small, oriented by hires or departments, that is recognized come Data Marts. The Data Mart is a multidimensional oriented data structure by hiring or departing from the organization that normally you can focus on the financial, commercial and marketing areas outgas (Kimball et al., 1998). The time of conception is ever shorter, allowing, at a later stage, the aggregation of different data Marts has a very broad structure, recognized by a philosophy

Bottom-up. Many organizations are now available as an option for building a Data Mart as a way to safeguard technological inexperience.

If the process in a specific area is concluded, I know initial evolution initiatives for other areas and more subsequently.

According to Malinowski and Simonyi (2009), the planning and construction of a data warehouse using a top-down philosophy is an effort considered in terms of customers and time, depending on size and level of complexity. Since the option of building a smaller sized Data Mart makes it impossible for organizations to recover it decided, once the investment to realize is substantially inferior, as well as time consuming.

The option of building a Data Warehouse or a Data Mart is now related to the needs of final users, from

Specific business needs and experience help organize this type of event. Many organizations

We opt for a Data Mart as a way to get ripe Algoma and provide visual results in a short space of time.

Less investment, which allows you to move forward for others departments with the highest level of delivery? In the meantime, a perspective of the Data Warehouse at the level of organization must not be an option to place on the side, since it offers a view.

To be organized as a whole, to the detriment of fragmented viewing of Mart Date.

For the size of the companies we are looking for and according to the theme yes, the selection of a data structure at the right level is not justified. Organization If so, the proposal will be returned for construction.

An information infrastructure oriented towards the financial area, as a special phase of our accounting data.

Data Warehouse Architecture

Return to the option and begin the data processing process view to or devolution from the analytical component, the two data operational systems are transferred through processes extraction, transformation and storage of data (ETL – Extract,

Transform and Load) to a central repository that allows.

Arrange large volumes of data, in an organized form, and conduct relevant analyzes on them. No ETL process.

The "Extract" phase occurs first, which means the collection or availability of different dice repositories (for example

In dice bases, archived in text format, calculation details and other data sources) for a temporary area, designated by Staging Area.

After the "Extract" phase will take place the "Transform" process represents the transformation of the original data into a group, Summarization", ""sanitation" of data in determinate format. The conclusion of this procedure is usually long complexity and volume of dice to deal with I don't feel this.

The stage must occur in a different environment between the systems operational.

Upon completion of the process of transforming the dice, these will be stored on the appropriate tables, depending on the form or

"Load" process. Its simplicity, or process of de-loading of dice is close to the existence of formed dice.

The design of the Data Warehouse will have to respond to how the organization will analyze the data and how it will try to fit the analytical systems in its structure. Entre so squeaks mains.

Known, the model in the extreme or the Star Schema responds to Interleague between the central fact table and the different tables of supports. Other data organizations are known, it is the model the snowflake or snowflake pattern as you explore sub dimensions of the different tables that attach to the central table factors.

The fact table identifies as factual numerical measurement represented. Each medium represents an intersection of all dimensions. For example, a consultation of an item from the Facts List table results in the extraction of various dimensions related to this information.

The selection of the model conditions the perspective that it is intended to give No sizing of the dice, or there may be one possibility more adequate analysis and reference of the data.

Analytical process

Originally, the analytical process was designated

As Multidimensional analyses may be performed on the data, Online Analytical Processing (OLAP) can be used to find a conjunction. TO growing importance of analytical component linked to or powered by

Visualization leading organizations to adopt a combination of data exploration techniques including sophisticated data mining techniques which combines statistical techniques for exploring large volumes of data, with the implementation of alerts that allow them to be proactively attentive associates to implementation of ad hoc analysis, with a view to greater understanding of priests unknown.

To start exploring the dice, in order to respond to different ones.

These are not the same as those addressed by customers, such as products most/less commercialized, at a height of one year, between others,

These, you can encourage and increase pro-active come

Seen as a result to the detriment of responsive and descriptive actions of the dice.

One of the latest developments in BI was the introduction of the concept of Corporate Performance Management (CPM), also I know how Enterprise Performance Management (EPM) or Business Performance Management (BPM), which is witnessing a development of the applications, methodology and technologies we provide help, plan, prevent and accompany all planning strategically linked to objective objectives. Como principal destitute this methodology is used to optimize the performance of the results by organization, through comparison of the results with the meats established (Hornbeam, 2006, Turban et al., 2008).

A growing trend in the form of Oldham's organization of data and the way in which he employs visualization techniques, methodology and procedures for obtaining information, in a manner to transform it into a solution, and which represents an advantage important competitive, I have no interest in the same way as organizations realize our own investments new technologies.

Viewing of dice

An exhaustive analysis of different reports, maps and other sources this information requires you to remove and implement as you would real and current practice among organizations to support people decided.

These are the tools used to achieve the best strategy to adopt and it is in this context that the idea arises and the need to aggregate all the relevant information in a single pain Quick, immediate and accessible reading.

The selection of relevant information is not always consensual to one person

As varied, analysis indicators or identified alerts

As such, they may be different in each organization and, within the organization; they may also be different from area to area, in the function of each sector or in the need for analysis, just as for different analysis sites. If I don't hear it, it's convenient

Each organizational area has a "control panel" suited to your analysis and management needs.

Once you have selected relevant information, it will be necessary again

"Just in time" availability, otherwise it will be different necessary to make the same or the same decision putting problems' answers into practice as quickly as feasible. This is when the Dashboard emerges. Or dashboard of a car, of an airplane, in this game, we provide much crucial information. Informants sober the speed, at which we move, the distance covered,

Using the Dashboard in the BI context allows you to view it at once consistent and integrated with all corporate information organization and organization of each of its areas, helping to monitor I leave this aside and optimize my decision making process. Neutrons cases, can be used to epilate or replace other aboard corporate relations. When directed towards communication, it may be placed on a single page, allowing you to eliminate customers associated with multiple software products.

As the main benefits of using hardware is nature's deistical-se:

a) A reduction in information dispersion, once in a while from a pain it passes to concentrated information;

b) Increased interaction capacity between us users;

c) The gesture is based on the indices and indicators that work as a reference;

d) Availability of information in "real time";

For its use in informed decision making e adequate;

Ease of access to information;

The ability to be adjusted and customized for use within the organization.

Economic-Financial Analysis Components

Many organizations regulate its economic activity dispersed operational systems. A majority of the systems Transactions may not be prepared for analysis.

Explorations, or when it becomes necessary to model and aggregate the data Different repositories in a single centralized data structure in a specific size, to support dynamic exploration.

For Acton and Cleaner (1991), a Gestapo ambition disprove information is quick and in greater detail and precise. The information of the accounting systems can be revealed opportunities to improve the quality and experience of you organizations, exploring your strong points at the same time

There you can have the opportunity to control your pinto's fracas, allowing them adapter e daiquiri with greater ease mordancies and Gestapo.

To understand the accounting elements, through analysis count on Balance and demonstration of Resulted, or ask me combination of the rubrics that can be used to remove the relationship economic-financial grandeur, designated as such economic, financial and operational indicators, among others,

It allows an evaluation of the strategies to be followed at any time.

The exact data and the actual details the information is undoubtedly relevant to your daily affairs organized in general. Among the two magnificent items positioned there.

The strategic gesture is to discover relevant information within the scope of historical information, which is not simple enough without suitable hardware as BI can provide.

Usually small and medium organizations are available in the pouch Analytical information armed in a structured and passive form it will not be used to support decision making. No intent, possess accounting nature information, invoice.

A few circumstances, product stock management, and other pertinent natural history information are included.

These dice poem be residents locally in the establishments of large organizations, in our cases, as an example for accounting information,

You can be located outside the company, once in a while PME do not have their own accounting cabinet, resorting to contract with specialized external services.

General and analytical accounting

The accounting geneses is explained – according to the main points authors – for the felt need for the home of Preacher as memory deficiencies, through a classification process and I note that it would allow you to easily record subsequent variations of certain magnitudes, so that at any moment it could happen knowing its full extent.

For Padoveze (2006), accounting is necessary and useful for as organized, in such a way that it is possible to conduct operations of any entity successfully over a long period of time there are limited possibilities of success. To stop starting registration reminder operations, an accounting of production information on the business level as a whole, which allows you.

Managers understand the current economic and financial situation exterior. The tax regime for the income of collective goods (IRC), by Decree-Lei nº 442-B/88 of 30 November, after

Article nº 115º (actualized for article nº 123º by Decree-Lei nº 159/2009 of 13 July), states that.

The tax regime for the income of collective goods (IRC), by Decree-Lei nº 442-B/88 of 30 November, after

article nº 115º (actualized for article nº 123º by Decree-Lei nº 159/2009 of 13 July), states that "As companies trade or citizens in a commercial form, as cooperatives, as public companies and as many entities that carry out, in their main title, a commercial, industrial or agricultural activity, with headquarters or effective management in the Portuguese territory, as well as entities that, although they do not have headquarters or effective management in that territory, are possible.

This establishment is required to have accounting available. Organized our thermos by you commercial and tax that alum dose requirements indicated no. 3 of item 17º, permit or control of profit taxable" (Portugal, 1988).

As far as the Tax Code is concerned on the Weights Return Singulars (IRS) through Decree-Law nº 442-A/88 of 30 of November, on the 28th article in line 2, includes the simplified regime for passive items that do not have a volume of sales exceeding 149,739.37 Euro, in these felt, for a volume of sales superior to these upright, are required to be available organized accounting.

The general accountant provides us with the economic-financial situation global company, in its external situation (sharing and responsibilities, among others) in accordance with the instructions legacies (Borges et al., 2000). I record the operations and other facts assets are currently governed according to an official plan Accounting (POC), agreed with the "accounting principles generally acuities". Started in full force on 1/Janeiro/2010 again.

The SNC adoption system is included in the accounting harmonization strategy of the European Union.

From continental model, basic no tax obligation limitation, for a reporting purpose Finance directed by external decision makers, which is practical current in the Anglo-Saxon model, it will produce effects in the form of carrying out and carrying out accounting on all the levels, which is why accounting is done, or which is looked at by the Official Accounting Technician

(TOC) a greater emphasis and knowledge of business activity,

Ask your contractor to have more information about his activity.

General accounting is not always provided with adequate information and regular periodicals. I don't feel it; accounting analytics describe another type of information, named after economic optics. Checking your customers and your results products, functions, and sections, and possibilities on the other side they will be as expected at the same time that allows you to know them devious entre other aspects, complementing this form to lack of information from general accounting .

Some authors like Marcos et al. (2001), refute queue an Analytical accounting is a method for effective implementation Gestapo control, carrying, is an instrument of forecasting and de I check it. As Pereira and Franco (2001), refer to the fact that analytical accounting must provide information that allows you to measure the "performance" of responsibilities at different levels of the organization. It is possible to analyze the results on the menus, by center of the customers and others separated from the information.

Establish the origin and determine the causes of the fluctuations verified.

The Balance

From a financial perspective, Balance trades is a set of applicators and capital originals that affect a determined entity. On the left side we see the representative elements of the applications of capital, namely, applications in fixed capital and applications in current capital. No direct confirmation of the representative heading of sources of financing said applications, name, social capital, results obtained in the exercise of business activity, bank financing, bakery credits, from the State and from other creoles, the passive (Rodriguez and Samos, 2008) .

The active fixings are tanginess (new designation adopted by the SNC compliant with Portugal (2009)) is linked for a long time an extended organization that is typically better than a person.

Recommend in this column a component of buildings, vehicles, machinery and financial investments among other things. Businesses do not have fixed applications for stays of less than one year, as with retailers, as divided to receive customers, or VAT to be recovered

From the state, the cash values and the bank deposits within columns.

The sources of financing for the applications increase nowhere directed balance, and, in addition to the fixed assets, there is a permanence time greater than a year. Normally, this element or social capital consists of liquid results and results transited between others. As a short lunch at the bakers, to the state in the form of VAT, the jointly contracted loans of financial institutions, among the creeds, are designated by passive.

Demonstration of Results

A temporary demonstration to highlight the results (profits or benefits) achieved in the activity involved in the company.

The gases carried out, starting from the organizational exercise, are the customers of the sold materials, the gases with the person below form of salary, or cost of supplying water, electricity for to activity and more auxiliary rubrics to decompose me Tormentor a member of the organizational guests.

The receipts (renditions no SNC (Portugal, 2009)) are tested in the financial and operational transactions of the organization generate value, which is a consequence of organizational capacity to create I negotiate. The difference between the recipes and the food is highlighted operational result.

Generally accepted accounting principles

The registry processes used, which were initially sufficient simples, forum-se generalized and refined, tendon charade as we have sorted out what is designated by the method accounting. This method is made up of a combination of registers relative to the magnitudes that we intend to observe and the variations augmentations and diminutives that we can suffer from.

Currently, the processing of business accounting information is assured by a vulgar accounting professional designated by the Official Counting Technician (TOC), with competence for your treatment and uniformity which will subsequently ensure communication with the State. The TOC may be external

Organized or not, if the organizations are obligated to

It is feasible to have a certified accounting firm that is well-organized and compliant with accounting standards. This principle of normalize and collect the tax returns as soon as I receive them recognize the necessity of existing principles, norms and procedures, which are of general application for all organizations, with the legal obligation of periodic presentation by accounting.

Regular practice of this activity is recommended for specific entities competent nationals, who are found in the Official Plan of Contabilidade (POC) queue currently represent as Norma's Accounting of Relate Financier (NCRF), e secure okras quested.

Not contemplated, it is also recommended and accepted by an organism international, or International Accounting Standards Committee

Financial analysis

A variety of options for the availability of the business manager, through medicine from the financial and economic component of the Management decisions made in the past, proven to be efficient in the pursuit of investment, operations and financing policies ago long time ago our organizations. Canted, look for the answers as questions "if the company's profitability satisfies expectations, if the financing schools should be carried out prudently among other questions, we can give you an objective and clear answer through financial analysis.

According to Helford (2002), there are many tools to implement the validation of business development, so we must bear in mind that the school of different techniques is almost always conducted by very specific value medicine. Moldavia, only some relationships

According to Naves (1992), financial analysis is a basic process a set of techniques that help you evaluate and interpret the company's economic-financial situation. Summer evaluation and interpretation center on these fundamental questions for survival and corporate devolution like this:

The financial balance;

- Capitals return ability;
- Or growth;
- Or I'm sorry.

This process is fundamental for different interested parties the management of the company, namely managers, creoles, trabalhadores e sues organizations, investitures State possibly customers.

The financial function, unlike other business functions,

It implies a forecast of future considerations, so that the financial functions are based on the future. This is the fact that comes back it is essential to integrate the dimensions, time and risk into the function financier (Gerard, 1992). Understanding the finance function

An organization inevitably returns to analyzing information sources basics, how to see the balance and demonstrate the results,

I am always ignorant of the reality of the demonstrations of the flows caiman, which contributes to a good treasury management.

The need to square historical accounting data as essential element for understanding evolutionary analysis organizations, time encouraged managers to use hardware statistics and visualization techniques of dice, with intuition meet disappointed masters. No anyway, it's not possible understand the evolution of organization without being attentive to us Demonstrators financers and as radios otiose a partier dresses dice.

Ratios

Some medical units are needed to validate them financial or business performance conditions.

The ratio system or indexes that link the component are used financial information with the operating data. The correct interpretation of the reasons gives the analyst or manager a perception financial conditions or business management (Bragg and Burton, 2006).

Generally, the reason expresses a relationship of greatness between two values in the form of a quotient or a percentage relationship (Gill e Catton, 1999). The clearing of assets in financial analysis, based on the

Accounting data of companies is a recurrent practice in the analysis of asset de-emphasis, assessment of accounting, management control, credit analysis and estimate of the disk market between other aspects (Naves, 1992). Moldavia, There are some limitations that may circumvent its use,

Like seam:

The wheels should not be considered in order aspects

Qualitative, as well as the ability to manage and motivate the functions, among others;

Comparing the stocks with the average values of the same sector may lead to certain inconsistencies, whether Please note that they must be used with some precautions;

Clearance of assets at the time of accounting

May not reflect the evolution of the organization over the long haul time, if it reflects a photographic view and not a film of the contents;

Another factor in consideration is a comparison of the stocks expected in the same period; otherwise, the effects of wisdom can lead to erroneous conclusions and decisions.

Para Gilman (2002), existed aide outgases precautions tar reconsiderations:

An analysis of a single index is not generally provided sufficient information to enable the organization to proceed globally. However, if the analysis focuses solely on specific aspects of the financial position of a company, one or two factors may be sufficient.

The financial data used must meet the same criteria appreciation. To use different criteria, especially In relation to stock and depreciation, it may distort resulting from analysis of stocks.

Among the aforementioned restrictions, there are, at the same time, countless factors that limit its use, without impeding the risks of constitute a valid instrument for control and aid in management. Examining the financial, economic, and operational factors in accordance with the business goals is important.

Financial considerations

The financial companies are columns that value component that relates exclusively to aspects.

Financial structure, investment quality, organization, valuation level, and investors' ability to make investments are all considered aspects of solvency. Financial companies can continue to do so following classification:

Activity radios same as efficiency and empress no its production cycle;

Radios debt aura the indices of sharing and respective capacity of the hurt face; Profitability ratios are available to you organization to generate profits and remunerate the action;

Liquidity rates calculate liquidation by company and others respective capacity to make compromises;

Package prices estimate the level of appreciation from organization attributed to the capital market.

The finalization of the financial indicators may be completed internal or for external entities, as for example, for customers, traders, analysts and investors among other stockholders. TO Comparing the stocks, with businesses in the same sector, may be a way of assessing the business balance faced by the rest.

In the meantime it will be possible to induce a limited analysis. Another way to establish a comparison of the desired races at the moment, the Optimally, it is to proceed with a historical analysis from the same place, to ascertain whether the medicines applied for a long time are suitable as a performance financier registered.

Solvabllity   =

Liquid situation

Passive

Autonomy Financier

Liquid situation

Active

After the autonomous purification of the ratios, evolution analysis from organization, in periods of years, through analysis of variations give greater explanatory and immediate power.

And Burton, 2006) the medicines adopted over a long period of time.

Operational reasons

The operational aspects favor the analysis of the organizational exploration cycle. Through the clearing of payments, the average payment period (PMP), the average payment period (PMR) and the average payment period of stock, among other headings,

Managers can validate the efficiency of the decisions in the management of the two recourses applicators.

Medium payment time

Suppliers Purchase

X 36

If there is no PMP ratio, if no PMR, the result is expressed on a daily basis. No case of PMP, a low value indicates a low level of financing reduced; being able to reveal a lack of permanent business capacity so sues suppliers. This analysis must be carried out jointly with the PMR account, which indicates the business relationship with you clients. Please confirm these two headings together detection of any unbalanced events. On the other hand, a comparison with the average of the sector can only provide data merely indicative; limiting this form to its use, devoid ago discovery initiatives evades a film peal Gestapo.

X 365 die

Middle reception area

=   Customers   X 365 dies Vcda

As a conforming expositor, radios financiers of operation give us a series of readings that we are probably going to advise the organization Gestapo to perform.

Existed, canted, outgas forms that can assist in the organizational management that we pass, for example, for the economic, economic-financial, among others.

Analyzes of specific characteristics of the activity in which it was inserted to organizations. For example, if a company with a group of cars could be interesting to think about the proportion of fuel gases in the parcel of all customers, in this case harm to the total combustible gas historical analysis. % Fuel Gas

=   Combustive

External Services Providers

This form of analysis gives a broader view of the parcel of fuel gases, or if the variation in the value of the gases could be used to increase the fuel consumption, or reveal the increase in fuel consumption, or an increase in sales,

Among other aspects, or what cares for a crusade analysis like other indicators that express other facts or circumstances.

A safe and confident analysis of financial demonstrations, in the interim of stocks, is recommended:

Do not analyze the isolated form; having to do as much as possible can be associated with other indices;

Consider a longer period of time for analysis, for this reason has been analyzed optically by its evolution;

Compare the organizational quotas with other companies

Finally, the use of equipment to monitor corporate activity is a recurrent practice, subject to unavailability from.

Accounting information, for organizations that can

Accounting under the outsourcing regime, it will be possible to constitute more than one.

Engrave in valence ad performance impresario.

Business Intelligence for SMEs – A prototype for accounting information

The option of developing a prototype may be an efficient method to validate the requirements of a project, as usual.

Detect any errors and discrepancies made according to the requirements project. In a Business Intelligence case, the prototype allows you to validate the capabilities of this technology through access to data and analyzes that can assist your decision-making process organizations.

To use the accounting data, it is not within the scope of a prototype that exemplify and clarification of applicability from Business Intelligence com accounting information, as vector impulse or of Smaller organizations, constitute an important point in the connection between the theoretical and practical understanding of using the hardware to make decisions. An exploration of the historical facts accountants such as BI hardware will facilitate the tomato.

Decisions and planning of relevant long-term extractions, through the use of visualization techniques of the dice and mechanisms for exploring large volumes of data,

Strengthening analyzes to disconcerted parents, or those who constituted an important advantage in understanding the business processes.

The proposed prototype will help you explore accounting information to transmit to the business managers to be applied by BI; naps organized in a general way, and reveal its importance management of modern organizations.

The concept of the prototype should be considered for the realization of the technology national business needs to find a solution small investment that the generality of the organizations can be accepted and used, as a way of leading to the improvement of the performance at the decision stage, through the increase in quantitative thermos and qualitative economic-financial information. No encasement from situation referred to and no establishment from apostate das PME me Business Intelligence solutions, through encouraging the use of Analytical hardware, or prototype is only a vector.

Potentially dynamiting organizations, thus exemplifying the advantages of using accounting analyzes later in management.

After the construction of the main goals of the prototype, we will follow if as different stages of study and devolution, than that

Deistical as follows:

An analysis of system architecture, as a form of identification.

As machines, as people, as information flow, as processes and to-do or immersive memo;

Selecting the development platform, which consists of one?

Learn from the program language and the infrastructure of the program adequate dice bases; • Analyze the main options of the prototype; as usual evaluate the main needs of development;

This is how users can access the prototype ea preservation of the confidentiality of the data;

Construction of the dice bases and tables necessary for this support accounting data, as well as transforming data for the analytical process; • Validation of the accounting data reporting method is not possible prototype;

How to transform and store the received dice

(OLTP) and carried in an analytical format (OLAP);

Analyze the analytical data using techniques

Explore and view data cubes (dice) in different formats. Upon completing the development, we will conduct various tests and validations to ensure the accuracy and reliability of the prototype, without exceeding the specified requirements..

Data Warehousing Process

The construction phase of a Data Warehouse in any one Organization is an important stage that comes from using of the data are not the analytical component of any company, one.

Instead, it involves transforming a large volume of data into a systematic structure, so that it is possible to implement it in our organizations.

Regardless of the size of the organization, an initiative of Business Intelligence comes in, among various elements, or designed construction of a Data Warehouse that ensures user satisfaction objective gestures.

By the size of the organizations in this study, and by the current situation in which many organizations now exist in our country results, failures, shipments, among other factors.

Unfortunately, one of the first management methods adopted is sometimes drastic reduction in investment in new technologies.

In this context, it may not be justifiable for a system transversal of BI that covers global organization, then

It is unlikely that there will be any organizations interested in the effect investments on a large scale.

From the perspective of finding Data Warehouse solutions that Satisfaction with minimum investment and results immediately emerge as best as possible to build a Data Mart oriented towards the financial area (Rasmussen et al., 2002), approving accounting information that organizations

Can be installed or removed, no need to be accounted for insured under the subcontracting regime. Most companies opt for subcontracting the accounting service provided to them elevated internal loads required for its maintenance.

The main problem identified in the Data Mart concept. Accounting for PME's is a multiplicity of accounting applications available on the market, with defined source code, without any need to implement ETL processes on them dice. I feel it, to fill inflexibility when I grow up most accounting packages are essential unwinding of an option that allows, in the first instance, oriented towards the financial area (Rasmussen et al.,

2002), approving accounting information that organizations.

Can be installed or removed, no need to be accounted for insured under the subcontracting regime. Most companies opt for subcontracting the accounting service provided to them.

Elevated internal loads required for its maintenance.

The main problem identified in the Data Mart concept.

Accounting for PME's is a multiplicity of accounting applications available on the market, with defined source code, without any need to implement ETL processes on the dice. I feel it, to fill inflexibility when I grow up most accounting packages are essential

Unwinding of an option that allows, in the first instance,

Tar accessing the dice, the same things that remain unbalanced, or that It allows you to shorten the aggregation process from data sources.

The structure of the data that serves as an interface between the accounting. No matter what the chip data is, they can be integrated from a simple monthly period to several months. Relatively to "Column", accounting information may be added to it numbering of two digits or more or what possibility other level of analysis. Ascertained or layout, the dice are important for the prototype, which will carry out the required validation and hygiene, maintaining this shape in consistency of the dice.

Modeling of accounting data

An accounting provide us do is instruments fundamentals Para an asset analysis of companies, balance and demonstration of results. The balance provides or situational awareness patrimonial, in a determinate moment of time, constituting itself

It feels like an aesthetic document, a photography experience. Show that the company itself (patrimony), must and that they must (divide) given by its elaboration, for the purpose.

Composed of Active, Passive and Proper Capital.

A demonstration of results shows a relationship between customers and testers, and how loses and let us go again.

The combination of these two character management instruments static surge or sizing from temporal information more widely, which allows, through visualization techniques and exploratory actions, an analysis most suitable for organization long time. In order for this accompaniment to be effective, it will be necessary to prepare data to support an analytical system and thus access a multidimensional analysis.

Or dosing supply data for the Business Intelligence system depends on its level details required for the analytical component, no minimum must be provided start from 2 digits (count the balance of the 2nd number), continue with one number corn detailed of contras possibility of a transfer corn details of the oscillations of the sub-counts, if at all, a level of Low corn granularity available for corn analysis particularized. On the other hand, it is possible to do so details; it allows you to carry out the aggregation of the same two, losing the level of tormentor more by consuming the thermos of interpretation.

The table of counts above presents an illustrative example of how you can identify and separate the combined counts of the balance and as count where the launches occur. This separation allows you to select the contacts you need for cleaning the items and how columns that can provide more detail from the accounts.

Data Warehouse Architecture

The model adopted for building the Data Warehouse is Star Scheme. I deviate from the size of the prototype, I designed it Implementation of the Data Warehouse solution in the Star Schema. This solution is based on the existence of a central factual table.

Or balance as many times as possible through the Entity tables, Periods, Counts, and Customers that we assign to the component dimension. The entity table contains information for users of the prototype. To use the prototype press up a prior application and acceptance of the conditions of use, being also required identifying the member.

The Customers table will contain information additional from the Current Account Customers column, allowing for a Multidimensional exploration, more in detail, from customer directory.

A connection between the identification of each customer, the sub-contacts from the Current Account Customers directory and the association from the table multidimensional Customers and Period, possibility of analysis behavior of organizational business processes. Summer analysis, in order to constitute a variant of financial analysis, It will allow different departments to organize to implement it conformity with this information.

Prototype infrastructure

The architectural design of the prototype is absent from this possibility organizations whereby we are able to account for the regime of subcontracting. A large majority of organizations resort to subcontracting the accounting service, due to the high levels of customers associated with its development and maintenance. Subsequently, availability of information accounting, analytical optics, is limited to existence or non-existence business development control maps in our different applications.

Of the accounting professionals who are authorized to develop and to send to the message for the fiscal administration.

Adina no follow-up from subcontract, to information search.

This gesture is a reality in the PME, without flowering or a theme from infra- technological support structure. To fill the need that organizations can provide evolutionary support for financial demonstrations; the prototype allows reception from information on a specific layout in text format, ensuring this form is more compatible among the different.

Communication from information within the accounting offices and the prototype will be performed on a web platform, or you can receive data from different platforms and this form supports your decision.

Accounting, analytical optics is limited to existence or non-existence business development control maps in our different applications of the accounting professionals who are authorized to develop and to send to the message for the fiscal administration.

The productive environment or the financial information source (OLTP) will be possible be in an accounting office or organization, far from the administrative location of the prototype, if only a remote connection is necessary and, once signed and authenticated, it will be possible to carry out all operations permitted on the prototype, as follows:

Defining the metrics/indicators of management;

Define the measurement parameters; Create users who can access the data; - Calculate and correct the accounting data; - Proceed to monitor the dice.

Tools to support decision making and viewing.

"In the Battle of Aljubarrota a situation of inferiority of recourses, or recurs to defensive strategies in a capacity to hope to truly reveal fundamental. However, this posture implies avoiding being worried about the importance of monitoring of course to compete and be able to have a strong leadership, capable of command rapid and decisive movements".

The strategy for using accounting data is not supported here Strategic decisions is a reality used by organizations large dimensions, same communication with different players

In the market, you have to be close to the data in the management, which normally has its own accounting cabinet within the organization. No case of PME's, mostly dos

Accounting data is outside the organization, as a consequence outsourcing from accounting, or which circumscribe or use of it information for the actions.

Full use of the data visualization capability, which is inherent in Business Intelligence hardware, allows for intuitive and rapid reading of accounting information and management steps. In order to obtain all historical information, all the data appear integrated, or what allows the managers correlate and reconcile the different numbers of dice, simultaneously, come Clara vantage competitive).

The interpretation of the accounting data, in conjunction with the evolution of the accounting.

Data confers greater explanatory power on evolution of business management. Many organizations are not available financial management support, or what could constitute.

Entry for external and internal business managers.

Benefit of use of financial information, linked to graphic exploration and multidimensional accounting dice.

Integration of Business Intelligence in an SME – Action Strategy

The companies operate in a dynamically very complex environment that requires a great deal of agility and prow-activity in our decision-making processes,

Or which involves understanding the information given in order to control it of form sustainable or future considerations, being this factor determinant that leverages many organizations to adopt BI measures and systems in their business processes.

In my opinion, and in particular, PME prefers to consult for information unless you make large investments.

As great organizations that present larger and larger structures hierarchical we can present some difficulties in adapting to the conditions of the market, returning to the vulnerability faced by organizations that are more flexible to changes as is the case of the PME's which, meanwhile, present other problems of shortcomings, consideration in sectors where size is a critical factor success (Dias et al., 2007).

Para Tonic (2006), the use of BI can have a great influence Medication shaped like the accountants realize their business.

Regardless of the form in which the information is prepared, the facts are historical and reveal the past, nevertheless, it information, when properly used, can be proven reveal the future. Or objectively analyze the demonstrators financers is auxiliary to the management through comparison, analysis and validation of the trend, as it is possible to predict the future from organization.

The ease of carrying out a historical analysis will be made easier if a organization can have a repository of historical data, internally queer from external source (from other companies, public dice bank, among other sources), which you can explore using BI techniques.

How Business Intelligence organizations can integrate powerful hardware in the case of business management with different analyses, mastered and ad-hoc relationship processing, management system monitoring of variable metrics, integration of data, panes de information and many other functions, all within one architecture oriented for services indispensable for a good corporate governance that orients us managers provide strategic direction for quality information, with the establishment of standards and processes that ensure the compliment of the objectives.

Come a Business Intelligence, as organizations can be understood in a systematic way information on sales and guidance on commercial policies for them specific needs of customers, allowing further investigation new and loyal old customers with quality products increased, as sustained.

Conjugation of historical accounting data with hardware of BI will allow PMEs to make relevant strategic decision through techniques explored in large volumes of data, enhancing analysis of unfamiliar teachers, which constitutes an important advantage in understanding the business processes.

Starting at the level of the data, different levels of aggregation and desegregation are obtained which allow for different character analyses. Further decompositions, through the hardware of the double list dice. No scope for decision-making, economic-financial data you can't leave it alone. Continued, through analysis and visualization techniques, you will be able to detect previously ignored evolutionary data. Therefore, as strategic measures, it will be possible to create training with specific character starters tactical, away from rigorous fixation of goals and objectives to attack them every moment, allowing or controlling it more simplified.

Mesas and corrections are more effective than the previous ones.

Critical factors of success

In a generalized form, loam managers for a business Intelligence as a management tool only accessible to great organizations. Moldavia, as PME's also possible as

The same reasons, this is, analyze the information available and achieve the greatest test of the based on the survey carried out at 510 organizations that implement initiatives related to BI, concluded if this:

61% of businesses consider themselves leading a company time;

59% of respondents said they received a single payment from truth;

57% of respondents consider that they contribute to one improvement das strategies e planes;

56% believe that there is a feeling of happiness following their decisions tactical ship;

55% say they have improved efficiency processes;

37% considering that a customer list is verified;

36% consider that customer satisfaction is improved;

35% say they are happy with their employees; As a result, 33% say there is a feeling of happiness.

No ROI (Return of Investment)

After recognition of benefits ad Business Intelligence, The organization will have to prepare the main lines for it to happen it is possible to lead the strategy from PME to the sense of orientation, or sea:

Engage and focus on all different efforts intervention who contribute to the persecution of the two organizational objectives;

Engage mouse managers to mitigate risk factors maximize implementation success;

Building a prototype will help you "sell" your idea.

And to demonstrate or alliance from Business Intelligence;

The organization must to develop accost with the supplier from BI solution that allows good management of the project, of form to reduce investment losses.

Assam, based on the size of the organization in the cause and an financial capacity to realize investments in this area, or objectively it will pass through the determination of the hardware/applications

Necessary to perform or drill-down the data, extract and monitor there are key indicators that allow us to monitor a company in shape efficient and rentable.

Strategic alignment

Organizational strategy alignment for various processes existents, provide a long-lasting vision.

Organizations must not lose sight of it, as it is about always having available resources to achieve certain objective objectives. The strategy, as a process, is answered in the same way will be planned as activities by organizations for persecution two objective objectives established by the company's policies. Nesses In this context, the strategy must offer a visual perspective horizon of action for an organization.

Chandler (2009), states that there are many organizations that try to fully implement a strategy that indicates a basic organizational orientation. However, in many situations, the strategy created is inappropriate, communicated in form disabled and faced with inadequate medical criteria. A process of alignment of strategy for action helps as organized to synchronize strategy with tactical activity,

Nuka conjuncture of economical financial crises, associate ago climate of globalization and mordancies globalism and regionalism (Will, 2008), mites

Organizations opt for hibernation, hoping to be better every day.

The strategy of "hoping for the truth" may never be the case advice once that customers will tend to increase their face try to retrace your sales, or you will end up in many businesses with an accumulation of a combination of unfavorable situations that will be difficult to reverse.

Organizations must adopt a reactive strategic behavior:

Adjusting the offer to your customers, for new introduction services and products;

Exploring a more competitive pricing model;

Substituting the current market for new markets;

Returning-if ever competitive against its rivals.

Looking at the PME, by Russo (2009), the principles of management strategy must follow the following word:

Need for a clear definition of direction/orientation from PME;

Deep understanding of the business in which it is

Inserted; Need to ensure balance between objectives operational a short prize, eon development and SME a long lunch;

For this purpose, ensure agility and flexibility through Learning new knowledge, adapting to it strategic and operational planning process.

Initiatory organizational strategic thinking if you use the analysis of opportunities, advantages, weak points and strong points (called SWOT analysis - Strengths, Weaknesses, Opportunities, Threats).

This analysis serves as a basis for reflection above

As competitive advantages and is built for competitive play from income from organizations in a general form. As companies they are required to adapt to sartorial and other realization memo evolving determinism

Definition of objectives and goals

The temporal horizon of objectives and goals is normally ever shorter that the organizational strategy. Normally, the objectives are correct established for a period of one year, which can be divided on a monthly basis, quarterly, semi-annual or other departments I agree with the business criteria. To fix the objectives and goals there are some steps, which we can vary the organization by organization, in consideration:

For all organizational areas, it must be objective

Of a long time, which provides a future vision of who you are it demands to be filled, and of medium/short time, which allows it to be maintained a He calls aces ago the language of the times (Boardman, 1997).

Associate objective metrics with quantitative and qualitative research metrics, assigning meats to these metrics (Turban et al., 2008).

Construct a diagram that allows you to link the objectives and goals set to the strategic objective of the organization, which you can quickly understand the interleague.

Engage and understand the objectives in every data human are ad organizations (Pang et al., 2008).

All people in a determined organization contribute to execute the strategy, through your daily activities, regardless of where we occupy the hierarchical structure. For someone to execute activities aligned with the strategy it is necessary to understand this strategy,

It involves a complex process of widespread communication to area employees Control and evaluation of the decision-making process.

Once you define the objectives and goals, you have to check the deviations from the basic metrics and follow the corrective actions.

Sung, many PME debated with a great insufficiency of information that allows you to effectively control defects. One information system that responds late as needed gesture, does not respond proactively to deficiencies, but before reactive form as events.

As seen by performance sago learned based on vision and organizational strategy. Do Follow it, the success factors are in agreement with you expectations created by customers, and by intervenient, as the intuition to provide a vision as a whole for organization and factors that influence its evolution. In the third place, as doctors there must be a limited number of critical factors of success. Fourth, the medical system must reflect, as much as possible, a cause-effect relationship so that interpretation is immediate. Ultimately, a medical system must be one communication hardware and strategy implementation organization.

The normal practice of organizations that focus on information is only the least favorable situation analysis, since this analysis is a reactive action to a negative situation. However, under the circumstances that the results are positive, the organizations do not carry out any changes, however, we must continue to evolve.

Please note that we can examine and optimize the results even further othiosis. This is a prow-active perspective from management.

Reactive focus

The reactive focus implies an action (or not) after analysis and response to a satisfaction or satisfaction. Habitually, as organizations analyze information and corrective medical measures pervading adversity.

Toad energy is exhausted by reactive organizations, which has detrimental effects on reversing poor outcomes and hinders the development of skills and chances. With these skills and business approaches, as organizations cannot validate "the noise of the trades".

On the other hand, Pang (2008) argues that the reactive strategy is passive. The organizations do not feel competent to act in support of disasters or protests. Even when some problems arise, denial is the first form of defense.

Osaka, a need to act is not always internalized by many people cognitive not as a practical norm.

The reactive management maintains the entire organizational structure constant state of alertness and anxiety. The metrics are correct frequently installed from the top to the bottom, from the viewing point give manager.

Business practice and reality are centered on the analysis unfavorable events, that is, if we are in the presence of one result inferior to or fixed, a perspective is to analyze what is wrong and place the organization in its entirety in the same direction occurrence.

Proactive focus

The person must decide whether to adopt a reactive behavior or not a proactive attitude. As organizations that apply legal measures pro-active setae vocation To connect opportunities.

For Kennedy-Glens and Schulz (2005), there were financial reasons why organizations must protect the pro-active Gestapo.

A proactive gesture is possible to anticipate the mistakes, or when they return less burdensome for organizations that support an attitude responsive to correcting problems.

We claim that the focus is above prevention of unproductive work and detection of problems original bridge. For this to be possible, communications within all areas of the organization must be concentrated on departmental necessities. Before exploring the advantages of proactive management if it is more economical, it must be taken care of by you Customs dresses devises. Once the whole organization is involved, from which the managers allocate all the resources to apply them Medias ate as workers queue realism us tribal, see measurements must be quantified. Since this is most important, it is important to organize yourself to ensure the consequences for your customers dresses devises.

Pang (2008), consider that a pro-active strategy ant eve as change institutions and stress to do more than what desperate. In order to support and sponsor these activities, consider this strategy as a source of diversity.

In summary, a proactive management system offers organizations In general, an effective, efficient and creative approach opportunities that are only revealed to those who are unfamiliar with it revalidate.

Applicability of the prototype not yet decided

It will be able to help you understand or learn from Business Intelligence naps organizations. However, these models do not pass through an exploratory action around some organizational data. The realized devolution could serve as an example for someone. Rear incorporation of a larger project.

The development of the project is important to your organization everything should be lined up as desired.

Among other aspects that require some future development.

Not what is rejected by the prototype, in order to substantially improve the analytical component, an aggregate analysis of topics and other categories arises, once it will be possible to "camouflage" aspects that we care about. This is, I return as an example to the practical analysis.

Average of receipts, which expresses the value per day, analyzed global will be able to express a value within two parameters normality, which leads the manager to think that it is not right to go back any corrective action.

However, a detailed analysis of my nature may reveal it

Aspects that care us of melancholy, that a less attentive manager,

It will not be possible to value it, because not everything is positive. Come suitable hardware in BI, a simple drill-down reveals less familiar aspects of its composition, or even if possible,

No concrete example, the breakdown by customer of the Radio Average price of receipts allows to validate which customer that you are not required to pay within the normal "intervals", and to develop.

Concrete steps to improve the indicator above all. If you are using a prototype of this nature, please fragilities that it presents, it is possible to be happy,

Require the manager to do as much of a global analysis as detailed of the available stocks.

Generally speaking, the traditional gesture is very focused on analyzing the least favorable aspects. Canted, a modern gesture must be every time you are less reactive, this is, "hope that I will meet you, then analysis", for a prow-active gesture that I explore as opportunities, if you are, absent in the actions that optimize you result.

In summary, the gesture is ambitious for easy reading information, short and immediate; however, the transformation of the data for the realization of an action strategy may require a flexibility of the information system that streamlines the process of decision, for what the majority of the systems still is not deviously preparation.

Analysis and definition of metrics

Selecting and defining the metrics for organizing the organization.

It is a crucial phase of strategy and definition of the objectives that are demands stinger.

The information in the PME is very varied, which may be subject to select the metrics. Invariably, accounting information is present in all organizations, with the obligation to provide information to the fiscal administration. By using accounting information, the organization will be able to find out how to use mastered resources, which will affect operational component, financial, economic, or other assets that are most often adjusted to make by business.

After selecting the metrics, you have to define the goals to be taken, which are a reference for the manager, so that it is possible to monitor the objective results and make the necessary adjustments.

Checking the results

An easy-to-read information panel allows users to monitor the results of the measurement metrics example, which has previously been aligned with the objectives and organizational strategy. Or I send two results ensure that the system support system is fixed so that corrective actions can be taken in due time.

I conclude the desired action is that the gesture is more effective than which reacts based on our objective results.

It is not within the scope of fixing the metrics and making it matter, it must be Evolve more than once the organization can do so. No meanwhile, a monitor the objective results, make the composition and Interpretation of the headings may not be immediate. I don't feel it, it is it is important that users of this information are read and read. We understand the true meaning of its evolution.

Validation methodology

The methodology adopted to validate this dissertation; I tend in the objective consideration of the study, step by step to the definition of a strategy of the works to realize so that the same thing happens to a satisfying pace. Among the various assumptions that you expect analyze and respective form of treatment, deistical-seas quested of investigation, the selection of interviews, the way in which the interviews are drawn up and the duration of the interview, or the collection and collection method I register two dice, and finally, how serious is the exposure from information collected in this article.

See below to identify the entries/entities.

This is very relevant to the whole process that you are going through contact me as soon as possible for positioning and knowing the details intervenient in this case.

The work will begin in April 2009 with the completion of the surveys between August and September 2009.

Process interveners

I've been analyzed in conjunction with the tees orientate; I tend to me consideration of the essential points that I am trying to give responded, namely, if to Business Intelligence podrida.

Applied to PME's, if the accounting information is in accordance with the conditions to support decisions, among other particular questions that we can arouse interest and analyze.

As selected entities to support the test forum:

An Association of Equines e Medias Empress (APME), fur so much knowledge of the realization of national business technology, as the main technological orientations, and as PME.

We can take advantage of BI as a decision support hardware store. As questions answered by Dr. Joaquin Cunha, president of the Association, with the participation of Dr. Jorge

It will be from Exact Portugal, a company providing technological solutions for the BI area.

Form of contact and collection of dice

It will be from Exact Portugal, a company providing technological solutions for the BI area.

An Orem c Technical Officials de Contras (OTOC), representing accounting professionals, to understand.

In your opinion, there is no requirement for rigorous information or justification for judgments made using accounting data. Today interview with the presence of Chairman, Dr. Domingues of Azevedo, and from Consultora ad OTOC, Drab. Paula Franco;

An association National of the Jove's Impresarios (ANJE),

We promote the organizations in order to obtain information on them how we can stimulate the companies we intend to adopt BI measures to support business decisions. A preview,

I was carried out by the delegation from Lisbon and I was in attendance do Dr. Dias Coelho, director of the Association.

To define the entities to contact, it is necessary to outline them a strategy of approaching the direct responsibilities of the two organisms and shaped like the process of recovery and I register two data from the interviews. This process can be followed as follows.

Make sure you get peace of mind and harmony

The enquiries for the realization of the enquiry, from among you methods that can be selected here are:

Removal of the installation of organisms objectively to solicit a request;

Make a request by e-mail to request a request;

Contact us by phone and try to schedule a date with us interviewed;

Board directly or by appointment.

Among these, you opt to approach the interveners directly to ensure that rear contact in the summer is made easier. TO aboard the interviews you can take place in the conferences you have. May Miriam be present as speakers. Please contact me directly and with my consent Requested, formalized by e-mail or by contacting us via email establishment at a certain date, time and place to be viewed.

Localization based on the interview recommendations will be prioritized and implemented as installations upon request. I am faced with the difficulty of scheduling and to silence some of the interviews, you need to various things contact us to obtain a positive response from the interveners.

3rd stage recording the information collected for a subsequent treatment not within the scope of these, is also a situation that requires prior analysis. As interviews took place under a form of dialogue, or which is a form of speech of the same kind complex, connection felt, and with the agreement of the interview, a The video was recorded on a magnetic support. For tall, the following procedure continues.

Explain the interview or objectivity of the interview and its relevancies;

Understand the history of the life of the interview determine the presence or absence of competitions, individual skills and abilities;

Request agreement for payment of the request magnetic support;

Formulary these questions in a brief overview table, if it justifies;

Allow silence to be interviewed as objectively as possible space for reflex, if necessary;

Maintain internal control;

Obtain confirmation of the interview for a demonstration of prototype;

Encourage or encourage you to make your own contribution possible sweet spots from the prototype.

4th stage conclusive the survey, first step; send it to someone Note of appreciation to the contacts. Transcribed toads as interviews e systematized principal conclusions. Face it specificity of the answers to the questions asked, opt for Transmit all the responses to each requested institution, in certain situations it is necessary to support the responses bibliographic review.

Finalized the collection of the data, proceed with global validation of the data presentations made, in conjunction with the tees orientation, tendon-

I concluded that the collected dice were seriously enough to give I will begin writing this dissertation.

Investigation questions

The investigation questions are divided into four succors. A diversified experience of each participant will be enriching globally as different investigation questions.

Accounting frame work. The question is whether the knowledge of the intervenient makes it possible to use accounting information for business management. Not within the scope of management businessman, expects participants to be provided with information the quantity and quality of information available to you.

Support in making decisions, exploring the technical intervention.

Official information on organizational management

Before starting this group of questions and I tend to consider them In this case, a brief overview of the business was carried out Intelligence and its components for receiving responses.

We were as objective as possible.

A prototype demonstration was carried out developed and dos requirements for its use.

We expect you to hear the opinion of the participants who do not respond:

Advantages and disadvantages of its use;

An aspects chef suffers from malaria; it's easy for organizations to adopt this type of application. We find the generic questions that allow us to validate the technological future for the PME.

Results of the questionnaire

Either the result of the investigations into the entities was clearly positive, or which allows me to continue with the written dissertation.

Association das Equines e Medias Businesses

In the current context, PME's is most interested in the outside world maximum part of the investment made, to the detriment of realization new investments. Not in the scope of Business Intelligence, much PME's pounces team Algoma initiative Dessau natures. For the other side, oh

The supply market is practically non-existent, so it can be said that implementing a BI solution for PME's is an act of pioneering. The BI market is popular.

For large organizations, and will only broaden the scope of this offer when the summer market is saturated.

I do not care about the interest of this type of hardware for the operator of the PME's, exist two realities:

Those business managers who return to the decade of 70-80, that we prefer to have a responsible response for the analysis from realized by the company, and which provides the relevant data from table.

A new generation of managers, descending from the previous one, who is more trained, clearer and more attentive, who prefers invest our resources to obtain analytical information, am detriment of investment and returns.

However, there is a dilemma that is currently arising.

Related to the advantage of being able to use analytical hardware, when there is a possibility of a return that does not always provide the necessary information, as one is responsible for the same as the least necessary. The new management of managers is less interested in the overall functions, but more interested in them information for all.

As for the transparency of accounting information among organizations, the information explains the company's realization. A generality of this companies run by bank entities, without feeling the temptation to do so better information about your activity, or the possibility of improving the conditions for accessing credit. On the other hand, the opening of the fiscal machine causes a limitation on manufacturing by accounting.

A major consideration of SMEs regarding accounting under the outsourcing regime, however, it is not normal to support organizations in an optical manner from corporate management, we can exceptionally apply small and rare advice pintails. The intervention of the Technical Accounting Officers is only limited to treatment by accounting information as viewed on receipt by mesa ago State.

In relation to the prototype, if it is expected to evolve towards marketing, there are two areas that require the best:

Presentation of dashboards, diversification of assets and here is a presentation that makes it easier to use the site other aspects, which would lead an SME to adopt this model of business;

Another aspect is the breakdown of the accounting data

In the details, allowing you to identify the information with the highest level of information.

Model of business;

Another aspect is the breakdown of the accounting data

In the details, allowing you to identify the information with the highest level of information.

In relation to the advantages/disadvantages of using the prototype, there are three points to consider:

The TOC available for information on the current prototype corn clients;

Availability of information on the prototype or customer to question with greater regularity and place these most diversified items in the TOC, which are evidently not prepared to give an answer;

Using the prototype allows pressure on the TOC to be achieved better at the customer's business reality, once again confined to the administrative activity of carrying accounting information to enter the country.

Ask for receipt of import from BI to PME, as

BI hardware stores serve, by tradition, the great organizations that we need to consolidate dispersed information. Nuka PME, EST.

Reality cannot be verified. The current concern of the PME Council is central the evolution of the sales, confirm that you are checking the major ones oscillations, which are the markets that have the best conditions for purchasing products, and this is achieved by Business Performance.

The main and great trend in the next few months is in thermos information technology, located at the level of BPM, once again.

The manager will always be receptive to find out the evolutionary pace from organization to the detriment of the progress of financial assets.

Similar posada team. Which refers to what can help organizations to optimize the results of their business through financial efficiency, human resources and matter?

The BPM foundation is absent BI. BPM is a new generation of applications that integrates from planning and controlling the management processes. For alum propose to the organizations a link between all the plans ago Operational level linked to strategic level, controlling

Customers arrangements with continuous monitoring of the goals objectives and adjustment if necessary ensuring the organizations overall decision making process is simple possible how to do it maintenance.

Finally, as PME specifies innovation, more confusion continues innovation with transformation. In Portugal, as organizations in general, we need to innovate in trading processes, especially on a high ground where we are going through a great moment,

There are some things that organizations need to abandon, so to speak how:

Focus on the solvency problem.

Strengthen the sales and put them all together. It's not enough, no more. You have to guarantee sales, but sales are in a way that guarantees liquidation.

Check how to achieve a potential economical solution,

☐

Orem of the Contras Technical Officials

The evolution of the procedures for filing the tax declarations by electronic means, with respective proofs and proofs this order is substantially reduced to manufacturing from accounting information that the organizations provide fiscal administration. As much as possible from bank entities like this others interested in accounting information, or who are solicited.

These are the tax declarations that are included in the demonstrations financiers. The company "producing" information with the aim of paying fewer taxes, is likely to jeopardize the result of the financial demonstrations that it lends to the banks, which is supposed to be the best organization. I have heard, there are two situations that we are both in conflict, or what levers companies to lend us to.

More real information from the organization. The technological evolution from tax administration limited to manufacturing ad information accounting. No meanwhile, the organizations will always provide forms of paying less imposed, but within legality, or which also affects the matter of bank credit and financial conditions, named as a legal tax, bank guarantee among others, which the banks can carry out credit operations.

Num decide businessman come PME, a cases de recourses humans connected to internal cargoes by an official technician.

Count (TOC) in the organization, we know the main reasons we are raising organizers to opt for an external TOC to implement it accounting, devoid as customs inherences. For the other side, employer, to delegate this responsibility to an external TOC, equally delegates to worry about the timely and correct supply declaration to the fiscal administration. Canted, this situation could happen outrun repercussions at the level of gestures, or disconfirmation of the two benefits from using information from financial demonstrations for the gesture. There is, at the same time, a growing trend organizations request financial information more regularity ago TOC numb perspective businessman,devoid a does aspects:

A pass age for the international regulations is obligatory something analyzed for which TOC is not prepared, or

which obliges to provide more information for the management and to talk more with the employer, provoking this form growing interest among employers to be better information about its organization;

The benches exercise a paper fundamental to this process, because you should request more support and support from your employer benefit from business activity this form of melancholy Substantial no decision making process.

In relation to the prototype, to companies and especially to PME, there is a great lack of information. The fact of existence applications for a business party which deal with information accounting, and that the employer can take it as a dependency to produce this information return all the advantages.

On the other hand, the knowledge of the company's activity is frequently confined to the employee, who will be able to detect any anomalies more easily, since the TOC will be able to do not have this availability, and therefore require more rigorous treatment from information.

Intelligence can influence the way in which it is realized.

In summary, accounting information and financial demonstrations we provide many data for business management. Canted, and am especially as PME, we don't always resort to this strategy. To use this information requires prior treatment for you

It is possible to extract all the potential of this information, allowing positional to organize our desired step of management.

National Association of Young Entrepreneurs

For import from this, the accounting information has not been passed you may be associated with the manufacturing and will also be more susceptible pre-enchainment errors. Currently, the trend is growing automation of its processing and respective tax receipt a clear reduction from its handling. On the other hand, the fact that accountancy must be in its majority under the outsourcing regime confidant to its manufacturing, because it requires a more profound vision from customer activity, from your business, from management, from the technician.Accounting Officer (TOC) is not available, in most situations.

Increasing use of accounting information in management organizations, in a general form, assume in our days an absolutely fundamental emergence, or which resumes the passage of an empirical gesture towards a gesture with scientific concepts. On the other hand, constantly use the same tools

Opening new horizons without understanding business management, favoring organizations in the appropriate selection process availability parameters.

To a large extent the PME proves to be nothing aware. Para o potential ad Business Intelligence. Currently, the gesture is carried out in a traditional way, this is -if at TOC or Balance and at Demonstration de Resulted, or Balanced, and promptly, upon request from PME, request an economic analysis- -financier. Now, if we are in the presence of BI hardware, represents a giant step in the way of processing information,

These aspects as PME will be able to improve your way of dealing with transactions.

This is related to the prototype, as this type of hardware is for companies You will be able to have a different handling capacity than usual, because or outsourcing from accounting limits the management material that the TOC lends itself to its customers. Another advantage that you get how to use a similar application is strictly for information.

Check out our accounting packages, or you can directly observe the manager/ employee from PME for information which consists in accounting. The hardware stores of BI can help you manage the various perspectives of different sections, if you want leas rubrics aggregated or decomposed, and you can disperse them managers for other level of delivery for or what PME aide.

Let's not despair, not even for its realization.

Lastly, innovation is essential to PME, or it means that, for size, it is organized with a great flexibility in terms of decisions and movements that large companies size not possible. No while, per ante or market must adopt a more structured posture by applying a more specific gesture scientifically, allowing you to better understand the sector where it is inserted and validated better than your potential. Ago navel ad strategic, must teem it counts as your devolution options, this is, validate what you will be able to differentiate your competitors and allow them to obtain advantages at the market level.

Conclusions and recommendations

In hardware suitable for management, the truth is that the power PME trading is limited by its size and specific characteristics. The literature is unanimous in stating its advantages in the application of BI techniques in general organizations; however the practical examples encountered are only reflected in business cases of large dimensions. Foe come base mesa revalidates and in these limitations that arose from the idea.

Developing the BI project PME. Face the desire to remove this work immediately, a definition of a strategy and the different steps to it conclusion constitutes the aspect most relevant to the whole process development from theses.

Thus, between the main stages or phases, the greatest significance for the completed project to be seen:

A decision on processing and subsequent development do prototype in a Web environment;

A methodology of investigation supported in the literature e direct inquiries;

Or shield ad Business Intelligence, General accountability

Analyze financial naps organizations me general queue permit enquirer generically or shield; and finally, the importance of being able to have a good strategy defined for or controlled by business activity, which It works as a type of connection between the two hardware and management hardware.

For completed queries, please note that they are applicable by BI for PME there is no common consensus, while there is no general acknowledgment of positive effect from BI which does not support the decision.

Likewise, for the demonstrations of the prototype that we are looking for realized, aboard realized with accounting information foe considered innovative for the generality of the entries. Canted, let's consider that the new prototype requires a certain melody Substantial at the level of the graphic image and information that it is available, to stimulate business and commercial interest in this type of analytical solutions. Our cases, as demonstrated.

Once realized, we can collect some ideas that we can enrich future developments of emerging information

Platforms.

The respondents were unanimous in affirming that the manufacturers of Accounting software can also make our dreams come true applications, an optics with an analytical component, given that it.

The alteration would constitute a key to the marketing of the product and, on the other hand, it would be available to SMEs for the possibility of using the product and better information that allows you to manage your business.

Entered into force by the Accounting Standards System,

It will be possible to create an increase by using the hair counts different stockholders and it will be possible to reveal a new one important in the quality of information. The use of accounting information to support decisions in time is useful one of the essential aspects in which the organizations and the cabinets accounting must be done jointly, to be able to do so

Success of your objective and strategic goals.

Close the perspective of what is happening on the component.

Finance of companies, it is not possible to ignore the form of information analysis, or if it is, the intact activities that are related to innovation and

Development com so Recourses Humans e com a Good will's entre other factors, which are not currently the subject of analysis shield.

Really, it's important to be able to have a good strategy

Defined, clarified and approved by the entire organization for this purpose we are looking at the objectives that the organizations are aiming for.

In fact, both goals and objectives must be adequate as much as possible to the available resources, so that all the returns we are happy and adequately affectionate. Ember a revalidate ad Business management is always reactive without control and correction unfavorable situations, proactively explore the opportunities.

In fact, both goals and objectives must be adequate as much as possible to the available resources, so that all the returns we are happy and adequately affectionate. Ember a revalidate ad Business management is always reactive without control and correction unfavorable situations, proactively explore the opportunities.

You will be able to position the organizations with our results.

As the last point, and I don't really want to specialize without a theme from Business Intelligence for PME, from the interviews conducted and the opinions of various authors, there is an enormous potential in Corporate Performance Management (CPM) in the near future of organization in general, what emerges as a recommendation for future work, or tested by CPM applied to PME nationals.

I conclude this with the expectation that the reading of this article has contributed to the understanding of how

Small and medium organizations can use accounting information to improve the conduct of their business.

www.ingramcontent.com/pod-product-compliance
Lightning Source LLC
Chambersburg PA
CBHW071059240526
45471CB00016B/2158